A Book of Angels

Written By
Karima Sperling

Illustrated By
Alia Nazeer

Other Titles By This Author:

My Little Lore of Light
The Light of Muhammad
Links of Light: The Golden Chain
The Story of Moses
Who Are You? A Book of Very Serious Questions
The Animals of Paradise
The Animals of Paradise: Coloring Book
My Little Lore of Light: Coloring Book
Every Day A Thousand Times
Ibrahim Khalil Allah
As-Salamu 'Alaykum Ya Rasul Allah (sas)
Animal Salams
The Family of 'Imran: Mary, Jesus, Zachariah, and John

As always this is dedicated to Mawlana Shaykh Nazim al-Haqqani and his Hajja Anne, who gave us so many beautiful stories to enlighten our way and to whom we owe more than words can tell.

And to Haniya, Humayra, Layka, Ishaq, Jacob, Hamza, Ghalib, Khalil, Noura, Karima, Tarik, Hala, Musa, the one on the way, and all our little angels.

Copyright © 2020 by Karima Sperling
All rights reserved. This book or any portion thereof may not be reproduced or used in any manner whatsoever without the express written permission of the publisher except for the use of brief quotations in a book review.
Printed in the United States of America ISBN 978-0-9913003-9-6
Little Bird Books littlebirdbooksink@gmail.com

Table of Contents

Introduction.. 5

1. Israfil (‘alayhi s-salam)... 11

2. Jibra-il (‘alayhi s-salam)....................................... 17

3. Mika-il (‘alayhi s-salam)...................................... 23

4. ‘Azra-il (‘alayhi s-salam)...................................... 29

5. The Angels of the Throne (‘alayhim as-salam)..... 36

6. The Rooster of the Throne (‘alayhi s-salam)......... 41

7. The Watchers (‘alayhima s-salam) and the Writers (‘alayhima s-salam).. 47

8. Angels Teach Us Our Religion............................. 53

9. In the Lap of an Angel... 57

10. Angels Learn Lessons Too................................ 61

Bibliography... 68

Introduction

The Messenger believes in what has been sent down to him from his Lord, as do the believers. They all believe in God, His Angels, His Books, and His Messengers. (The Qur'an 2:285).

We have been ordered by our loving Creator, Allah 'Azza wa Jalla, to believe in Him and to believe in His Angels, His Books, and His Prophets. His Books we can hold in our hands and read. His Prophets are human beings similar to ourselves who have left their perfect words and actions as a lighted path for us to follow. But His Angels are a special creation whose presence in our lives we are required to believe in and yet whose existence we can neither see nor confirm.

What Are Angels

Angels are beings created by Allah Almighty to inhabit the heavens and to serve as His messengers, conveying His commands to humans and to the rest of creation. They do not have flesh and blood bodies like our own. Instead they have bodies made of pure light. They are able to move about without the normal restrictions of time and space. They can travel far distances in the blink of an eye and they can be in many different places at the same time. They were made in all shapes, sizes, and colors. Some are similar to things we know and some are frighteningly different. Some light is glowing and warm, while some light, like a laser, is blinding and piercing. Angels are also able to change their shapes and take on a different appearance when necessary. The Qur'an (37:150) directly implies that angels are not female. When they take human bodies, as far as we know, they take the forms of men. However, they are both gentle and powerful spiritual beings with no need to be either men or women since they neither marry nor have children.

Angels live in the heavens but they visit the earth and there are many, many more of them than there are animals, jinn, and men combined. They are the most numerous of all creation. There is no place in all the heavens where angels are absent. The Prophet (sall Allahu 'alayhi wa sallam) said he could hear the heavens groaning under their weight. And all of them are perfect servants of Allah Almighty.

Although angels do not have physical bodies, they do have hearts and minds, thoughts and feelings. Their greatest delight is to worship their Creator. When they are not praying, they are glorifying His Majesty, His Mightiness, His Beauty and His Kindness. Angels do not have egos. They are never selfish or proud. They are never rebellious or disobedient. They do what their Lord wants them to do and their only desire is to please Him. They have no need to ask for forgiveness because their worship is perfect and they do only what they were created to do.

Because Allah Almighty ordered them to bow before our father Adam ('alayhi s-salam) they consider it their duty to be of service to human beings. They watch over us with worry and concern. As much as angels are mysterious to us because we cannot see them, so we are a mystery to them because they can see us, and the mistakes we make. Because we were made with stubborn, independent wills, we constantly challenge our Lord, disobey His laws, are unthankful, and sometimes even forget Him altogether. The angels cannot understand this. It puzzles and upsets them so they pray for us and ask Allah Almighty to forgive us. Angels are our helpers and friends.

How do we know about Angels?

Sometimes we can sense the presence of angels with our hearts but that is not the same as really seeing. Mostly we must rely on what we read in the holy books and what we are told by those to whom Allah Almighty has given the gift of sight and wisdom, the prophets and the saints. They have told us about the things that they can see which we cannot. They have informed us about some of what they know of the realms of the unseen.

What follows is a description of a few of the angels who have the closest connection to us and the greatest involvement in our lives. We know about them from what is related to us by the Prophet Muhammad (sall Allahu 'alayhi wa sallam), the Beloved of Allah ('Azza wa Jalla), who was taken on the Night Journey to visit in person the heavens and their inhabitants. Because we love him and trust him, we believe what he has told us.

1.
Israfil
(‘alayhi s-salam)

Before Allah (‘Azza wa Jalla) created the world, He created the Throne. It is not a place to sit but rather it is the sign of His power and kingship over His worlds. After the Throne, Allah created the Trumpet whose sound will signal the end of the worlds that He was about to call into existence. He said to the Trumpet “Be” and it became. He made it out of translucent pearl with luminous colors reflected in an iridescent glow and He hung it on a scarlet cord from one of the posts of His Throne. Then Allah created the Archangel Israfil (‘alayhi s-salam) from the glorious light of the Throne. He said to him “Be” and he became.

He was the first angel created. After him Allah ('Azza wa Jalla) filled the heavens with angelic beings. The Prophet Muhammad (sall Allahu 'alayhi wa sallam) said that there is not even as much as four fingers of emptiness in the place we call space. In fact, you cannot move through space without stepping on angels. The whole universe is crowded with angels of every size and description praying and glorifying their Creator and carrying out His commands. Israfil ('alayhi s-salam) is the greatest and most solemn of the four archangels who serve the angelic world as prophets and messengers and he is the closest to Allah. There are only seven veils between him and the Throne of Power and his name means 'Servant of the Merciful'. He is so compassionate that he has not smiled, since the day the fires of Hell were lit, in concern for those of us who may one day suffer there.

The body of the Trumpet is so long that it has space for a separate finger hole for every person who will ever be created. This means that each of us has our own unique musical tone which is like our name and by which we will be called. The mouthpiece of the Trumpet is a hole so big that all the heavens and all the earths could fit inside and it is over this cavernous opening that Israfil (‘alayhi s-salam) will place his mouth and, expanding his mighty chest, blow into it to make it sound.

Israfil (‘alayhi s-salam) has four wings. One wing stretches all the way to the East. One wing stretches all the way to the West. One wing covers his body and descends down, down, down to the seventh earth where his feet are firmly planted. The fourth wing is spread over his head like a canopy to shield him from the blazing glory of the Throne. His face appears in the middle with eyes like two milky stars.

Because he is able to be in more than one place at a time, even when he is sent on other business, Israfil (‘alayhi s-salam) stands with his eyes fixed on the Throne, never sleeping or wavering. He is always poised in readiness and expectation. No one but Allah (‘Azza wa Jalla) knows when the time will come for Israfil (‘alayhi s-salam) to pick up the Trumpet and blow it to signal the end of the world as we know it. He must always be ready. He hasn’t moved or looked away since the day he was created for fear he might miss the command of his Lord. He is the angel of the Hour and in his hand is the “Mother of Books”, the original heavenly source of all holy books (al-Qur’an 13:39).

When the first human prophet Adam ('alayhi s-salam) was created, Allah ordered all the angels to bow before him, to bow before the light of Muhammad (sall Allahu 'alayhi wa s-sallam) that he carried. Israfil ('alayhi s-salam) was the first of the angels to obey his Lord's command and he bowed down low before our father Adam ('alayhi s-salam). For this he was honored by having The Holy Qur'an written on his forehead. When Allah writes His orders and laws, He writes them between the milky eyes of Israfil ('alayhi s-salam).

It is the job of Israfil ('alayhi s-salam) to hear Allah's commands and to transmit them to the rest of the angels. It is said that, as the prophet Dawud's ('alayhi s-salam) voice was the most beautiful among men, the voice of Israfil ('alayhi s-salam) is the most beautiful among angels. When he speaks or praises his Lord all the other angels stop their own hymns to marvel at the beauty.

When the day comes that Allah Almighty commands Israfil ('alayhi s-salam) to take the Trumpet from where it is hanging on the Throne and put his mouth over its mouthpiece and blow, in that moment the world will stop. The mountains will drift away like wisps of wool, the sun will grow big and close so that it scorches the shade-less flattened plain of the earth below it. As Israfil ('alayhi s-salam) blows each note, the soul whose name it sounds will arise from their resting place wherever it is. The body of each soul will pull itself together out of bones and dust and mud, and collect itself into the same form that it had when it was alive. Allah ('Azza wa Jalla) will order each soul to reenter its body and be born again. We will all come running to the call of our Creator with fear and with hope.

Israfil ('alayhi s-salam) is standing guard over us and praying for our welfare. We must also pray for him. Allah bless our master Sayyiduna Israfil ('alayhi s-salam).

2.
Jibra-il
('alayhi s-salam)

Then Allah ('Azza wa Jalla) created Jibra-il ('alayhi s-salam) whose name means 'Servant of Allah'. He is also called the loyal spirit and the favorite of his Lord. Allah made him from radiant light and made him more beautiful and more majestic than words can describe or imagination can picture. He has 600 wings that he spreads like a fan around him. All of them are pearly white and they extend farther than the eye can see in every direction. His hair is plaited in braids which look like strings of small pearls and on his head is a golden crown encircling a turban of light. He is dressed in a white silk robe that his Lord has decorated with all the jewels of heaven and earth. They glitter and glow so that

his face and form are clouded as though seen through a veil. Around his waist is a belt of pearls, each one like the full moon. From his wings hang beads of pearl and the soles of his feet are covered in green gems from which crystals dangle like drops of dew.

We are told that this is the heavenly form in which the Prophet Muhammad (sall Allahu ‘alayhi wa s-sallam) saw him twice, once in heaven and once on earth. When he appeared on earth, he filled the whole dome of the sky from side to side, from back to front, so that there was nothing to be seen but him. His head was like a mountain and the space between his two eyes reached from horizon to horizon. His chest was broad and it would take a bird 500 years to fly from one of his shoulders to the other. However, sometimes he can take the shape of a man who is just a little bit cleaner and a little bit brighter than an actual man. In this way the rest of us can see him and not be frightened. And, if it is Allah’s wish, he can even appear as small as a sparrow.

His home and place of prayer is in a hollow of the gigantic angelic tree called the Cedar of the Farthest Limit (Sidratu l-Muntaha) which grows by the boundless sea at the end of creation beyond which only the Prophet (sall Allahu 'alayhi wa s-sallam) has traveled. The trunk and branches of the tree belong to a stalwart angel and his leaves consist of uncountable smaller angels. When Allah ('Azza wa Jalla) wants to address mankind He tells Jibra-il ('alayhi s-salam) to gather certain of these leaves and give them to those He has chosen to be His prophets. Each leaf is a letter and together they spell out the words and sentences of Allah's books. The Holy Qur'an is made up of these leaf green letters, each one of which is a living angel whose shape and form must be read, recited, and treated with care.

Once or twice a day Jibra-il ('alayhi s-salam) plunges into the boundless sea. When he emerges, he shakes out his wings. From each drop that falls from each feather of each of his 600 wings a new angel is born. Five times a day Israfil ('alayhi s-salam) gives the call to prayer for all the angels. Jibra-il ('alayhi s-salam) or Mika-il ('alayhi s-salam) lead the prayer and on the day of Friday (Juma') Mika-il ('alayhi s-salam) gives the sermon.

Jibra-il ('alayhi s-salam) is Allah's messenger and he has been a help and a companion to all the

prophets. It is he who brought them revelation and he who gave them their books. It was he who first appeared to the awestruck Prophet Muhammad (sall Allahu 'alayhi wa s-sallam) in the night sky above the cave on Mount Nur, bringing the first lines of The Qur'an, "Read, in the name of your Lord who created." (al-Qur'an 96:1). It is he who woke the Prophet (sall Allahu 'alayhi wa s-sallam) again one starry night in the city of Mecca and, holding the reins of the angelic horse, Buraq, traveled as his guide to Jerusalem and then to the seven heavens. It was by the tip of his wing that the life-giving well of Zamzam was opened for Sayyida Hajar (radhi Allahu 'anha) and her baby the prophet Isma'il ('alayhi s-salam) and now for all of us. It was from his wing that the prophet Ibrahim ('alayhi s-salam) nursed when he was a baby hidden from the tyrant Namrud in the cave.

But Jibra-il ('alayhi s-salam) is also the one who hurls Allah's punishment on those who have earned it. It was his wing that shook the earth and overturned the cities of the prophet Lut ('alayhi s-salam), who were disobedient to their Lord ('Azza wa Jalla). And it was Jibra-il ('alayhi s-salam) on his white horse who enticed the armies of Pharaoh after Musa ('alayhi s-salam) to their doom in the sea. Jibra-il ('alayhi s-salam) commands vast armies of angel warriors riding angel horses, the long tails of their turbans streaming behind them like banners. They bring victory to the believers and terror to the tyrants. In the battle of Badr, the enemies of the Prophet Muhammad (sall Allahu 'alayhi wa sallam) were stricken with fear when they saw these angels and they ran from the battlefield shaking uncontrollably. Also under the command of Jibra-il ('alayhi s-salam) are the winds with which, when Allah ('Azza wa Jalla) orders, he deals out stern reminders and warnings to a rebellious, ungrateful mankind in the form of storms and cyclones. And it is Jibra-il ('alayhi s-salam) who, with the tip of just one of his mighty wings, causes earthquakes.

And all the while, in fury or in gentleness, Jibra-il ('alayhi s-salam) has no other concern in his great heart except to worship Allah and to be of service to us. So we must remember him and pray for him as well: May Allah bless our master Sayyiduna Jibra-il ('alayhi s-salam).

3. Mika-il ('alayhi s-salam)

Allah ('Azza wa Jalla) created Mika-il ('alayhi s-salam) from resplendent light by saying "Be" and he became. His name means 'Little Servant of Allah' although he is far from little. The place where Allah stationed him is past the outermost limit of creation and over the Sea of Mercy. He is one of the imams of the heavenly beings. The angels never stop singing the praises and glory of Allah, some of them standing, some of them bowing, some of them kneeling with their foreheads flat on the groundless air. However, when they hear the call of Israfil ('alayhi s-salam) they stand to follow as Mika-il ('alayhi s-salam), or sometimes Jibra-il ('alayhi s-salam), leads them in the five daily prayers which are just the same as the Prophet Muhammad (sall Allahu 'alayhi wa s-sallam) has taught us. When we pray our prayers on time, we are joining the angelic congregation.

Mika-il ('alayhi s-salam) holds in his hand the Book of Provision in which Allah Almighty has written every bite of food and every drop of water allotted to each of His creations on earth. Mika-il ('alayhi s-salam) makes sure that everyone gets what was written for them, not one crumb more and not one sip less. He has charge over the rain and the thunder. Under his command is an army of tiny soldiers called the Angels of Mercy. Some of them herd the clouds with long staffs just as if they were flocks of woolly sheep, directing them to the lands where they are needed. Then they ride each drop of rain to the exact spot on which Allah has intended it to fall.

As Jibra-il ('alayhi s-salam) is fierce, so Mika-il ('alayhi s-salam) is gentle. As Jibra-il ('alayhi s-salam) withholds, so Mika-il ('alayhi s-salam) extends. As Jibra-il ('alayhi s-salam) punishes, so Mika-il ('alayhi s-salam) nourishes. But Mika-il ('alayhi s-salam) is a warrior also. It was Jibra-il ('alayhi s-salam) on his great white angelic mare who enticed Pharaoh to ride into the sea following Musa ('alayhi s-salam) and who made sure that the tyrant died unforgiven in an avalanche of waves. But it was Mika-il ('alayhi s-salam) on his piebald charger who chased Pharaoh's army from behind to make sure

that not one of Musa's ('alayhi s-salam) enemies was left unpunished.

Mika-il ('alayhi s-salam) is the guardian of all the living things on the earth. He watches over the plants and the animals and he watches over us. He is aware of every leaf from the time it begins to swell on its branch, to the time it withers and falls to the ground. He sends his tiny soldiers of mercy to gently open every bud and he takes delight in every bloom. He is intently watching every sprout that springs from the earth and every weed that sways in the sea. He watches over the wild animals in their burrows deep in the earth and in their nests high in the trees. He watches over them and makes sure they receive exactly what Allah ('Azza wa Jalla) has written for them. His angels keep the birds from falling from the sky and the fish from drowning in the sea. They make sure that the squirrels land safely on their branches and the cats land squarely on their feet; that the delicate butterflies find their winter shelter, the determined salmon their birthing places, and the dusty elephants their watering holes.

Every living thing has at least one angel from Mika-il's ('alayhi s-salam) army of mercy that keeps it company and keeps it safe from the moment of its creation to the end of its life: every stone, every leaf, every snail, every ant, every grain of rice, and every drop of water. So we must respect these creations and their angels, not kick them with our feet or destroy them for no reason. We must eat all the last bits of food on our plate or give them to another. We must pick up every crumb that falls and not let the work of any angel be disrespected or go to waste.

The wings of Mika-il (‘alayhi s-salam) are white, tinged with green, and his robe is green, the color of living things. His face is full of kindness and his light changes colors rapidly like a dancing rainbow. He has seen the fires of hell and he is a witness to the weakness of men. He will hold the balance scale on the Day of Judgment and he wants everyone’s good deeds to weigh heavy.

As Mika-il (‘alayhi s-salam) cares for and nurtures the beautiful world around us and protects us from evil so we should also remember and pray for him. Allah bless our master Sayyiduna Mika-il (‘alayhi s-salam).

4.
'Azra-il
('alayhi s-salam)

'Azra-il ('alayhi s-salam) is the fourth of Allah's great archangels. Allah ('Azza wa Jalla) made him by saying "Be" and he became. Perhaps his place is behind the Throne since it is said that Jibra-il ('alayhi s-salam) is to the right, Mika-il ('alayhi s-salam) is to the left, and Israfil ('alayhi s-salam) is in front.

When the heavens were completed and filled with angels of every size and description; when the universes were spread out and strung with stars; when the earth was spun round, the dry land pulled out of the sea and covered with grass and trees for all the animals to live in; only then did Allah ('Azza wa Jalla) decide to make the very last of His creatures - mankind. He called His four archangels, His most obedient servants. First He asked Jibra-il ('alayhi s-salam) to go to earth and bring back a handful of dirt. But earth cried so hard at the thought that from her skin a sinful man might be made, that Jibra-il ('alayhi s-salam) could not do as he was ordered. So Allah sent Mika-il ('alayhi s-salam) but he also was unable to bear the tears of the earth and so he returned ashamed and empty handed. Then Israfil ('alayhi s-salam) was sent and even he could not get himself to take any piece of the pathetic earth. So Allah sent 'Azra-il ('alayhi s-salam) to fulfill His command. 'Azra-il ('alayhi s-salam) proved blind to earth's tears, deaf to her wails, and indifferent to her pleading. He obeyed his Lord without hesitation. He scooped some dirt of every sort from all over the earth despite her protestations and he brought it quickly to his Lord. To this handful of dirt Allah ('Azza wa Jalla) added some water from the rivers of paradise to make a sticky clay. From this clay Allah ('Azza wa Jalla) molded the first man, our father the prophet Adam ('alayhi s-salam), and from the little that was leftover He made the first date palm.

Because of his unwavering obedience, Allah gave 'Azra-il ('alayhi s-salam) a new

name. In The Qur'an the only name by which he is known is Maliku l-Mawt, the Angel of Death. It is his job to pluck the living soul from the body of every human being and every fish and every beast, bird and bug. He will do as his Lord wills, nothing more, nothing less, and he will not be swayed by the tears or fears of men.

Allah made him of a glowing light and clothed him in a white robe embroidered with jewels. For believers who are happy to return to their Lord, his appearance is beautiful, gentle, and kind and his arrival is heralded by the sweetest of scents. It is said that on his right hand Allah ('Azza wa Jalla) has inscribed the words, Bismi Llahi r-Rahmani r-Rahim - in the name of Allah the Kind and Compassionate. When the ones who love their Lord see these letters of light they work like a strong magnet to attract and draw their souls smoothly out of their bodies without pain and without regret.

However, 'Azra-il ('alayhi s-salam) can appear quite differently to those who are not happy to see him. He is as the one who sees him thinks him to be. So for those who prefer the world to the meeting with their Lord, he can be totally fearsome and grotesque. His entire body appears to be covered in eyes and hair. Each of his hairs looks like a person standing with flames coming out of his ears. His golden light is hidden by black blackness and his wings are like flames.

On the day in the middle of the month of Sha'ban Allah gives 'Azra-il ('alayhi s-salam) a list of all the souls he must take in the coming year, man and beast. 'Azra-il ('alayhi s-salam) sits with the earth spread out like a large shallow bowl that he holds between his knees. In one hand he grasps the list while with the other hand he rifles through all the living creatures in the dish to find the one whose name is next and he carefully picks them out.

Some say that 'Azra'il ('alayhi s-salam) sits beside a huge tree called the Tree of Life. It is covered in leaves smaller than the leaf of the olive. When any being is born on earth a new leaf with their name on it buds out of this tree and begins to grow. The person or animal grows with the leaf. When its time is done, the leaf begins to brown and shrivel. Forty days before their soul will be gathered, a person's leaf falls from the tree onto the page 'Azra-il ('alayhi s-salam) is holding and the name written on the leaf is erased from the list. There is no more provision written for that soul on earth. With no more food and no more water, they cannot live here any

more.

Like the other archangels, ‘Azra-il (‘alayhi s-salam) has many smaller angels working at his command and they help keep watch on all living things. But no one takes the soul of a human being except ‘Azra-il (‘alayhi s-salam) himself. This is his duty and he does it well. When he takes a soul he shows it both paradise, whose guardian is the angel Ridwan (‘alayhi s-salam), and hellfire, whose guardian is the angel Malik (‘alayhi s-salam). Then he puts the soul back in its body to await the Questioners, two blue-black angels by the names of Munkar (‘alayhi s-salam) and Nakir (‘alayhi s-salam). The Questioners visit the dead on the first night to ask two important questions: “Who is your Lord and who Is Muhammad (sall Allahu ‘alayhi wa sallam)?” If the dead one answers correctly, “My Lord is Allah, God of the Heavens and Earths and Muhammad (sall Allahu ‘alayhi wa sallam) is His servant and messenger”, then their small grave opens to become a spacious and fragrant garden from which they can see and enjoy the paradise that awaits them. The only people who will not be questioned are the prophets, the martyrs, and the children. They will be taken immediately to heaven.

‘Azra-il (‘alayhi s-salam) is one of the angels who is always around us. He keeps us company from the time

we are born until the time we die, visiting each living person at least twice every day. Somehow he is able, by the permission of Allah ('Azza wa Jalla) to be present with everyone at once, watching and waiting. The wise souls know him well and are comforted by his presence. He reminds them that one day they will return to their loving Lord, pleased and well pleasing. When the wise ones die they even miss his familiar company.

At the very end of time 'Azra-il ('alayhi s-salam) will be ordered to take the lives of all the angels since Allah has decreed that everything living must taste of death. All the angels will give up their souls to him one by one and then he will take the souls of the archangels one by one. Israfil ('alayhi s-salam) will be the last. Then Allah will take the soul of 'Azra-il ('alayhi s-salam) himself and so death will be the very last to die. After that there will be no death ever, only eternal life.

Allah bless our Master Sayyiduna 'Azra-il ('alayhi s-salam). May we only see him as he truly is, beautiful and shining, shepherding us to the happy meeting with our Lord.

5.
The Angels of the Throne (‘alayhim as-salam)

“And the angels will be on its sides, and that Day, eight will carry above them the Throne of your Lord.” (al-Qur’an 69:17). These are the Throne Bearing angels, called Hamalatu l-‘Arsh. Just as the Throne of

Allah is a mystery, so little is known about the angels who carry it. We do not know their individual names and we do not know for sure how many there are except, as The Qur'an tells us, that on the Day of Judgment there will be eight of them. So it is thought that before that day perhaps there are only four, one to hold each corner of the Throne but on the Judgment Day the Majesty of the Lord will be so great that there will need to be double the number of angelic Throne Bearers.

All the Throne Bearing Angels (as) are enormous and strong. Allah ('Azza wa Jalla) made them out of some of the light of His Throne by saying to them "Be" and they became. They carry the Throne on the backs of their necks and shoulders which forces their chins down onto their chests. The intense light of the throne and its immense weight prevent them from ever looking up. From the moment they were created they have been glorifying their Lord and asking His mercy for the inhabitants of earth.

One angel has the form of a strong young man and he prays "Holy are You, O Lord. Your glory fills the heavens and earths. Take care of all the human beings and look on them with Your kindness and mercy." One angel has the form of a golden lion and he prays "Holy are You, O Lord. Your glory fills the heavens and earths. Take care of all the wild animals." One angel has the form of a shiny black bull and he prays "Holy are You,

O Lord. Your glory fills all the heavens and earths. Take care of all the domestic and pasturing animals.” One angel has the form of a wide winged eagle. His prayer is “Holy are You, O Lord. Your glory fills the heavens and earths. Take care of all the creatures that fly and swim.”

They are so big that the distance between one corner of one of their eyes to the other is a distance of 500 years traveling. Their feet are at the farthest limit of the universe and their heads below the Throne. They always have their heads bowed for fear of looking at the glory of the Throne above them. They each have four wings two on their back with which they fly and two on their face to shield them from the light that surrounds them.

These angels are immensely strong and powerful yet they get tired under the weight of the Throne. One day they asked to take a short rest from their labor and were told to relax their hold on the Throne. To their amazement they discovered that they were not carrying the Throne but in fact the Throne was carrying them.

They pray for our welfare with every breath and we must pray for them also. May Allah bless the Angels of the Throne (‘alayhim as-salam).

6.
The Rooster of the Throne ('alayhi s-salam)

Above the Divine Throne is an emerald pillar which supports a dome of pearl. On the top of this dome sits an angel in the form of a White Rooster ('alayhi s-salam). He is the most magnificent of roosters with 500 wings, each of which has 1,000 feathers of pure bright luminous white. On his head is a forked comb of rubies the color of pomegranate seeds. At the times of prayer this Rooster ('alayhi s-salam) stirs himself. Slowly and with powerful majesty he shakes open, one by one, each of his 500 wings. The winds generated by this mighty movement cause the leaves of the trees in the gardens of paradise to flap and flutter and the flowers to bend and bow.

From each feather a drop of water, from one of Allah Almighty's oceans of mercy, falls making a gentle rain that mists the world below. The Rooster ('alayhi s-salam) raises his great head, opens his cavernous beak, and begins to crow. All the inhabitants of all the heavens hear his song and turn to each other and ask "What has happened? What is the good news?" In this way Allah Almighty lets them know that the time for prayer has arrived. Then Israfil ('alayhi s-salam) arises and, placing his right hand to his ear, he calls out "Allahu Akbar" to alert the angels to prepare themselves to join the heavenly prayer.

The people of earth hear nothing. However, all the pure white roosters in the barnyards and chicken coops do hear and they cock their heads to one side in order to listen more intently. Then they begin to flap their wings and to crow. The other roosters of various colors follow their lead and begin to crow also. This is how the people of earth know that the time for prayer has arrived. Those of them, who get up from their soft beds or stop whatever they are doing and arise to pray, are bathed in the rain of mercy that falls from the wings of the angelic Rooster ('alayhi s-salam). Those who continue to sleep or do not pay attention, miss this opportunity to bathe in heavenly light.

Allah ('Azza wa Jalla) loves the White Rooster ('alayhi s-salam) and He asks him the reason for his crowing, not because He doesn't know but because He wants the Rooster to make it clear and for the rest of us to hear. The Rooster ('alayhi s-salam) answers that his only wish is that mankind receives their Lord's blessing. Allah assures the Rooster ('alayhi s-salam) that at every time of prayer He looks down at His praying servants with His gaze of Mercy and promises them gardens in paradise. At that happy news the White Rooster ('alayhi s-salam) is satisfied and he settles his ruffled feathers and becomes quiet.

The Prophet (sall Allahu 'alayhi wa sallam) said he loves the White Rooster and that Jibra-il ('alayhi s-salam) also loves the White Rooster ('alayhi s-salam).

This has been the routine of the Rooster ('alayhi s-salam) on every day since the day he was created and it will continue until two nights before the last night. At that time when he begins to stir and shake out his wings, Allah Almighty will command him to be still and not make a sound. That night will continue for three days without the sun rising. Only those who were accustomed to praying will arise to pray and ask Allah ('Azza wa Jalla) to forgive them. After this very long night, the sun will dawn in the western sky rather than in the east where it has risen since its creation. Only then will people know that the last day has come.

So we should be happy to hear the roosters crow and run to do our prayer. May Allah bless the White

Rooster ('alayhi s-salam) who cares for us so much that he wakes us from sleep to bathe in the rain of mercy.

7.
The Watchers ('alayhima s-salam) and the Writers ('alayhima s-salam)

Allah Almighty has assigned to every human being on earth four personal angels. They surround us at all times, one in front, one in back and one on each side. They keep company with a baby from the moment it is first created inside its mother and then from the time it is born until it grows old and passes away. They never leave, they never fall asleep, and they never get distracted or bored. They do not know what it means to get tired and or to disobey their Lord. This is simply the way they were made. They do not have to choose between good and bad but they know the difference and they feel terribly sorry for humans who sometimes act as if they do not know.

There are two angels whom Allah Almighty assigns to a baby even before it is born. Allah tells these angels to record three things concerning the baby's future: how long it will live, if its life will be easy or difficult, and lastly, how much food and possessions it will be given to make use of. These angels begin protecting the baby inside its mother and when it is born they take up their positions one in front and one behind it. The two angels are called al-Mu'aqqibat, the Watchers ('alayhima s-salam). Sometimes they are also called the Guardian Angels. They make sure that no harm comes to the person in their care unless it is what Allah has ordered for them and is their destiny. No one can twist their ankle or skin their knee, get sick or die, unless that is what Allah has written for them at the time they were first created. No one can use something that is not theirs. No one can lose something they were meant to have. We must never feel that we missed out on something or that things could have been different. Things that happen are just the way they should be, although not all people act in just the way they should act. So we do the best we can and always try to be pleased with what Allah the Most Generous has written for us.

There is another pair of angels who are called Kiraman Katibin, the Noble Writers ('alayhima s-salam). **"Surely there are guardians over you, noble writers, who know all that you do."** (al-Qur'an 82:10-12).

There are some who understand the two adjectives used to describe them in The Qur'an (50:18) as their names, Raqib (watchful) and 'Atid (ready). Two of these angels are assigned to keep company with each human being from birth until death. Each angel has a book in which he is ordered to write down all the deeds, good and bad, that a person performs throughout every second of every day of their entire life.

It is said that the angel whose job it is to record goodness sits on the right shoulder and that the angel whose job it is to record badness sits on the left (al-Qur'an 50:17). From these vantage points each angel can see whatever a person does and hear whatever they say and even understand their thoughts. The Angel of the Right ('alayhi s-salam) records every kind word, every considerate thought, and every positive action and he writes them in his book, not once but ten times. The Angel of the Left ('alayhi s-salam) is supposed to record all the unkind, rude, and inconsiderate things but since he is under the command of the Angel of the Right ('alayhi s-salam), he is forbidden to write anything at all until he is given permission. If the person does something mean, the Angel of the Right ('alayhi s-salam) forbids the Angel of the Left ('alayhi s-salam) to write anything down. He tells him, "Wait. Maybe they will be sorry and ask forgiveness. Wait. Maybe they will try to undo the harm that they did." And so the Angel of the

Left ('alayhi s-salam) waits. He waits an hour, two hours, three hours. Finally, after six hours if the person has not asked for forgiveness, the Angel of the Left ('alayhi s-salam) is permitted to write it down but only as one bad deed.

It is also said that when a person tells a lie such a horrible stench comes from their mouth that the Angel of the Right can no longer keep his seat on their right shoulder. He has to move far away for a long time until the smell is gone. This means that many good deeds might be lost and not written down during his absence.

The books these angels write are not for Allah. Allah ('Azza wa Jalla) knows and sees everything. He needs no reminding nor help. These books are for us to read about ourselves, to see clearly what we did in our life and to be humble and grateful. Without the overwhelming mercy of our generous Lord we could never be good enough to deserve the gifts He gives us.

On the Day of Judgment, Yawmu l-Qiyamah, each soul will be handed their books to read and see for themselves the value of their life. They will read the book of goodness and be happy. They will read the book of badness and be ashamed. So the best is for us to be as kind, grateful, and considerate as possible and to always ask Allah ('Azza wa Jalla) to forgive us when we are not. In that way maybe we can keep the Angel of the Left ('alayhi s-salam) from writing too much in his book.

We must be grateful to our angels - those who keep us from the harm that is not written for us, and those who are most generous in the records they keep. Every time we end our prayer we turn to each side and say “as-salamu ‘alaykum” first to the Angel on the Right, then to the Angel on the Left. May Allah bless the Watchers (‘alayhima s-salam) and the Writers (‘alayhima s-salam).

8.
Angels Teach Us Our Religion

One day, Sayyiduna 'Umar (radhi Allahu 'anhu) reported that he and a group of companions were sitting with the Prophet (sall Allahu 'alayhi wa sallam) in the shade outside his mosque in Medina. A man came and made his way purposefully through the crowd. He sat himself down in a position of unusual familiarity that bordered on rudeness, face to face with the Prophet (sall Allahu 'alayhi wa sallam), his knees up against the Prophet's knees. His hair was very black and his clothes were very white. There were no visible signs of travel, no dirt nor dust nor sweat, on him and yet no one had ever seen him before.

The stranger said: “O Muhammad, tell me about Islam.”

The Prophet (sall Allahu ‘alayhi wa sallam) answered: “Islam is to say, ‘There is no God but Allah and Muhammad is His Messenger’; to pray; to pay zakat; to fast Ramadan; and to make the Hajj if possible.”

To the surprise of everyone, the visitor said: “You have spoken truly.” Then he asked: “O Muhammad, tell me about Iman, belief.”

The Prophet (sall Allahu ‘alayhi wa sallam) said: “Iman is to believe in Allah, in His Angels, in His Books, in His Messengers, in the Last Day, and to believe in the divine Decree both the good and the bad.”

Again the stranger said: “You have spoken truly.” Then he asked: “O Muhammad, tell me about Ihsan, goodness.”

The Prophet (sall Allahu ‘alayhi wa sallam) answered: “Ihsan is to know that even if you do not see Allah, He sees you.”

The stranger nodded his head once more and said: “You have spoken truly.” Finally, he asked: “O Muhammad, tell me about the Hour, the Last Day.”

The Prophet (sall Allahu ‘alayhi wa sallam) said: “The one being asked knows no more than the one who is asking.” Meaning that this is something that only Allah (‘Azza wa Jalla) knows.

The stranger then got up and went away. No one

saw where he went. After some time, the Prophet (sall Allahu 'alayhi wa sallam) said to Sayyiduna 'Umar (radhi Allahu 'anhu): "Do you know who that was?"

Sayyiduna 'Umar (radhi Allahu 'anhu) replied that he did not.

The Prophet (sall Allahu 'alayhi wa sallam) told him: "That was the archangel Jibra-il ('alayhi s-salam) come to teach you your religion."

9.
In the Lap of an Angel

Usually when Jibra-il ('alayhi s-salam) brought revelation to the Prophet Muhammad (sall Allahu 'alayhi wa sallam), even if others were nearby, they could not see him. Sometimes, however, the archangel would visit the Prophet (sall Allahu 'alayhi wa sallam) in a form that could be seen by everyone. He could not appear in his true form because it would be too frightening and overwhelming. Even the Prophet himself (sall Allahu 'alayhi wa sallam), the first time he saw Jibra-il ('alayhi s-salam), found it difficult to not be afraid of the extreme brightness and size of the unearthly figure of the mighty angel. When the angel wanted, however, to be seen he could take the form of a man. Usually Jibra-il (‘alayhi s-salam) chose to appear as the companion whose name was Dihya al-Kalbi (radhi Allahu ‘anhu).

Dihya (radhi Allahu ‘anhu) was a young man from a southern Arabian tribe who had begun as an enemy of Islam and had even fought against and killed some of the Muslims. But when he met the Prophet (sall Allahu ‘alayhi wa sallam) in person all that changed. Faith entered his heart and he loved the Prophet (sall Allahu ‘alayhi wa sallam) so much that he begged for forgiveness and offered his own life as payment for the harm he had done. Allah and His Prophet forgave him and he became a believing Muslim. He spent as much time as he could in the company of the Prophet (sall Allahu ‘alayhi wa sallam). Whenever he came to Medina to visit he brought gifts for the Prophet (sall Allahu ‘alayhi wa sallam) and for all his family including his two little grandsons Hasan and Husain (radhi Allahu ‘anhuma). Dihya (radhi Allahu ‘anhu) was a very handsome young man. He was even called the Yusuf of the tribe of Kalb because just as the prophet Yusuf (‘alayhi s-salam) is said to be the most handsome of all the prophets, so Dihya (radhi Allahu ‘anhu) was said to be the most handsome of his people and of the companions.

One day Jibra-il (‘alayhi s-salam) descended from the heavens to visit the Prophet (sall Allahu ‘alayhi wa sallam). He was sitting among the group of companions having taken the form of Dihya (radhi Allahu ‘anhu), when Hasan (radhi Allahu ‘anhu) and Husain (radhi Allahu ‘anhu) saw him. The boys made their way running through the seated companions until they got to Dihya (radhi Allahu ‘anhu). They jumped on his lap and playfully began searching in his robe and pockets, looking for the gifts and sweets that he always brought them. This time, however, it was not really Dihya (radhi Allahu ‘anhu) they were teasing but it was the archangel in the form of Dihya (radhi Allahu ‘anhu).

Jibra’il (‘alayhi s-salam) had never before experienced such an encounter with human children. He was confused and uncomfortable. He looked over at the Prophet (sall Allahu ‘alayhi wa sallam) as if to ask, “What are they looking for? What are they doing?” The Prophet (sall Allahu ‘alayhi wa sallam) smiled and explained that his grandsons were not being rude or rough, they were merely looking for the treats that their kindly uncle usually brought them. And so without knowing, the blessed grandchildren of the Prophet (sall Allahu ‘alayhi wa sallam) had been playing and tumbling in the lap of an archangel.

10.
Angels Learn Lessons Too

It is said that one day MIka-il ('alayhi s-salam) was looking down from his place in the heavens and he saw his favorite human sitting on a hill watching his vast flocks of sheep and goats pasturing on the slopes with their lambs and kids scampering around them. Down in the valley he could see thousands of his cows and horses absorbed in searching out the juiciest grass. On the other side of the hill camels in large numbers were standing with their necks bent to munch the wild herbs that grew there in abundance. The compassionate archangel frowned and his eyes became full of concern.

He went to consult his brother angel Jibra-il ('alayhi s-salam) who looked down and saw the same pastoral scene. He returned Mika-il's ('alayhi s-salam) worried look and the two of them went to consult with Israfil ('alayhi s-salam). His heart was also disturbed by what he saw and so the three brought their concerns to their Lord, Allah ('Azza was Jalla). They said: "O Lord Most High, we are so worried about Your servant Ibrahim ('alayhi s-salam). He has so much wealth and so many of the goods of this world that we are afraid he must have left off the remembrance of You and is spending his time working to collect more and more. We must do something for him before he loses paradise and eternal life in Your Divine Presence."

The Generous Lord answered them that He knew His servant Ibrahim, whom He had chosen above all others to be His intimate friend. But if the angels were so concerned, they had permission to descend to earth and take a closer look. So the three mighty archangels took on the appearance of three young human men and they went to do as their Lord had advised them.

Ibrahim ('alayhi s-salam) was sitting outside his tent one evening when saw in the distance three men on foot coming over the hills towards his encampment. He called to Sarah (radhi Allahu 'anha) his wife and told her they would be having guests for dinner, to light the oven and prepare bread. He told the herdsman to sacrifice an animal and put the meat on the fire to cook. All was ready when the three strangers arrived at the tent.

Ibrahim ('alayhi s-salam) invited them to eat with him and set the fresh bread and steaming platter of meat before them. Angels do not have material bodies and so of course do not eat food. In order not to reveal their true identity, they said that they do not eat unless they have lawfully paid for the food. "What is your price?" they asked. Ibrahim ('alayhi s-salam) thought and then answered, "The price is to say "BismiLlah" over the food before eating. The angel Mika-il ('alayhi s-salam) replied "Shall I tell you something even better to say?" Ibrahim ('alayhi s-salam) was surprised and told him to say whatever he thought could be better than that. Mika-il ('alayhi s-salam) raised his voice and in crystal clear notes he sang out "Subbuhun quddus rabbu l-mala'ikati wa r-ruh" - Glorious and Holy is the Lord of the angels and the spirit.

Ibrahim ('alayhi s-salam) was spellbound. Never in all his days had he heard anything that compared to this glorification of Allah Almighty. Never in all his life had he heard a voice so sparkling and pure. He forgot about the food growing cold on the platter. He forgot about hosting hungry guests. He just begged the stranger to please say it again.

Mika-il ('alayhi s-salam) wanted to test Ibrahim ('alayhi s-salam) to see how much it was worth to him. "If I say it again" he said "what will you give me?" Ibrahim ('alayhi s-salam), without a moment's hesitation, offered a third of all he owned if the stranger would only repeat his words once more. Mika-il ('alayhi s-salam) agreed. Again his voice rang out over the hills and through the valleys: "Subbuhun quddus rabbu l-mala'ikati wa r-ruh."

Ibrahim ('alayhi s-salam) gasped in wonder. He had no thought for anything now other than this beautiful phrase, this beautiful praise of his Glorious Lord. "Say it again" he pleaded. This time Jibra'il ('alayhi s-salam) asked him what he would give to have it repeated. "A third of all I own" the prophet replied. Jibra-il ('alayhi s-salam), in the voice that leads the angels in prayer five times a day, sang out from the depths of his great heart: "Subbuhun quddus rabbu l-mala'ikati wa r-ruh."

Could anything be more true? Could anything be more beautiful? Could anything possibly be worth more? Ibrahim ('alayhi s-salam) begged the stranger to say it again. This time Israfil ('alayhi s-salam) offered to hymn the praises of his Lord and asked for the same price. In the deepest most sonorous of tones that filled the valleys and echoed over the hills to the wide desert beyond, the archangel whose mighty breath will make the Trumpet of the last day sound, sang out: "Subbuhun quddus rabbu l-mala'ikati wa r-ruh" - Glorious and Holy is the Lord of the angels and the spirit.

His heart breaking, Sayyiduna Ibrahim ('alayhi s-salam) pulled himself away from his guests. He picked up his staff and he took Sarah (radhi Allahu 'anha) by the hand. He turned his back on his home and everything he owned to set off into the wilderness with nothing. The angels called after him but he only told them to eat the food that was rightfully theirs and to make themselves at home because it all now belonged to them. There was nothing in the world he wanted other than to hear the strangers repeat their praise but he had nothing left to pay.

At this point the angels realized their mistake. The prophet Ibrahim ('alayhi s-salam) had not forgotten his Lord, had not forsaken his Friend, had not traded his servanthood to be king of the world. They begged him to return and take back his herds and his herdsmen, his tents and his rugs, his water skins and his cooking pots, but Ibrahim ('alayhi s-salam) would have nothing of it.

The angels revealed their true identities. What use do angels have for cows and sheep? What use do they have for milk or butter, for servants or tents? Ibrahim (as) was not really surprised at their confession, he had felt in his heart that they were not ordinary worldly guests, but he would not take back one hair of one goat or one drop of cow's milk. What he had given away in the sight of Allah he could never be persuaded to take back again.

The angels pleaded to no avail. Ibrahim ('alayhi s-salam) began to leave with the faithful Sarah (radhi Allahu 'anha) by his side. The angels cried out to their

Lord to help them undo the damage they had done. Allah ('Azza wa Jalla) told them to tell His friend Ibrahim ('alayhi s-salam) that his payment was accepted but that someone was needed to pasture the cows and herd the sheep, to feed and protect the herdsmen and their families. The angels could not do this. Allah ('Azza wa Jalla) was asking Ibrahim ('alayhi s-salam) to be His shepherd, to watch His flocks and His servants as His steward. To this Ibrahim ('alayhi s-salam) could only humbly consent.

And so the angels returned to their heavenly stations, much relieved, having learned something important about why it is that they were ordered to bow before Adam ('alayhi s-salam) and the human prophets. Ibrahim ('alayhi s-salam) and Sarah (radhi Allahu 'anha) returned to their tents and continued taking care of the Lord's flocks while their hearts repeated the praise the angels had taught them. Only now they said: "Subbuhun quddus rabbuna wa rabbu l-mala'ikati wa r-ruh." Glorious and Holy is our Lord and the Lord of the angels and the spirit.

Bibliography

Adil, Hajjah Amina. *Lore of Light*. Washington D.C.: ISCA, 2009.

Adil, Hajjah Amina. *Muhammad - Messenger of Islam*. Washington D.C.: ISCA, 2002.

Adil, Hajjah Amina. *Forty Questions*. Washington D.C.: ISCA, 2013.

Burge, S.R. *Angels in Islam. A Commentary with Selected Translations of Jalalu d-Din as-Suyuti's Al-Haba'ik fi akhbar al-mala'ik (The Arrangement of the Traditions about Angels)*. University of Edinburgh, 2009. Accessed 2019.

Kabbani, Shaykh Muhammad Hisham. *Angels Unveiled: A Sufi Perspective*. Washington D.C.: ISCA, 1995.

al-Tabari, Abu Jafar Muhammad b. Jarir. *The History of al-Tabari vol. III. W. M.* Brinner trans. Albany: SUNY, 1991.

al-Tha'labi, Abu Ishaq Ahmad b. Muhammad Ibrahim. *'Ara'is al-Majalis Qisas al Anbiya or Lives of the Prophets*. W. M. Brinner trans. Leiden: E. J. Brill, 2002

www.ingramcontent.com/pod-product-compliance
Lightning Source LLC
LaVergne TN
LVHW052348100826
845147LV00012B/789

9780991300396